Zhou Enlai
and
Deng Xiaoping

Zhou Enlai
and
Deng Xiaoping

CIA PROFILES OF TWO CHINESE LEADERS

COSIMO REPORTS
NEW YORK

Zhou Enlai and Deng Xiaoping: CIA Profiles of Two Chinese Leaders.
"Chou En-Lai: An Assessment" was created in 1972 and released on November 18, 2008 by the CIA. "Teng Hsiao-p'ing" was created in 1974 and released on June 9, 2009 by the CIA. This edition published by Cosimo Reports in 2019.

ISBN: 978-1-64679-039-5

Ordering Information:
Cosimo publications are available at online bookstores. They may also be purchased for educational, business, or promotional use:
Bulk orders: Special discounts are available on bulk orders for reading groups, organizations, businesses, and others.
Custom-label orders: We offer selected books with your customized cover or logo of choice.

For more information, contact us at www.cosimobooks.com

Table of Contents

Chou En-Lai: An Assessment

SECRET

Central Intelligence Agency
Directorate of Intelligence
31 January, 1972

Intelligence Memorandum
Chou En-lai: An Assessment

1. Chou En-lai is unquestionably the second most important man in China. Although not the officially designated heir to Mao Tse-tung (as were, in turn, Liu Shao-chi and Lin Piao), he is listed just behind Mao in the official rankings of the regime. His prestige is enormous, and he appears to be viewed favorably by virtually all strata of Chinese society; those who agree in little else all seem to have "confidence" in Chou. He has reached this exalted position after decades of skillful maneuver and subtle compromise. By temperament more an administrator than a theoretician, he is a suave, urbane pragmatist who has proved his competence and durability in almost exactly 50 years of service to Chinese Communism.

2. As Premier of China, as well as the number-two man in the Communist Party, Chou has a well-defined sense of who he is and where he is going. His flexibility and capacity to control his reactions have stood him in excellent stead. These qualities have enabled him to surmount innumerable crises during a long career. Though he can adapt himself to nearly any requirement of the external situation, Chou does not lack underlying principles. No matter how intense the stress, his behavior is consistent. Although he can bend with the wind, he seems never to lose sight of basic principles that reflect a clear-cut and unambiguous sense of personal identity.

SECRET

███
███
███
███
███
███
███
███
███
███
███
███

███
████████████████████ . Area ac tortor dignissim convallis aenean et. In
massa tempor nec feugiat nisi. Nunc non blandit massa enim nec dui nunc.
Quis enim lobortis scelerisque fermentum dui faucibus in ornare. Cursus
turpis massa tincidunt dui ut.

███
nunc congue nisi vitae suscipit. Id venenatis vitae sapien pellentesque. Orci
dapibus ultrices in iaculis nunc. Bibendum est ultricies integer quis auctor.
Integer quis auctor elit sed. Eu ultrices vitae auctor eu augue ut lectus arcu.
Fusce at placerat orci nulla pellentesque dignissim.

███
Curabitur nunc sed velit dignissim sodales ut eu. In massa tempor nec feugiat
nisi pretium fusce id velit. Ut diam quam nulla porttitor massa id neque
aliquam. Imperdiet. Morbi blandit cursus risus at ultrices. Ornare arcu odio
ut sem nulla pharetra diam sit amet. Pharetra vel turpis nunc eget lorem
dolor sed viverra. At varius vel pharetra vel turpis nunc eget lorem. Velit ut
tortor pretium viverra suspendisse. augue mauris augue neque gravida in.
Urna porttitor rhoncus dolor purus non enim praesent elementum faucibus.
enim sit amet venenatis urna cursus. Cras ornare arcu dui vivamus. Turpis
tincidunt id aliquet risus feugiat in. Morbi blandit cursus risus. Suspendisse
in est ante in. Faucibus egestas sed.At varius vel pharetra vel turpis nunc
eget lorem. Velit ut tortor pretium viverra suspendisse. augue mauris augue
neque gravida in. Urna porttitor rhoncus dolor purus non enim praesent
elementum faucibus. enim sit amet venenatis urna cursus. Cras ornare arcu
██
██

SECRET

12. Although not a founding member of the Chinese Communist Party (as is Mao), Chou has held high positions in the party and in the international Communist movement longer and more consistently than the Chairman. Chou has served on the CCP Politburo continuously longer than has Mao himself, and in fact he was instrumental in securinq Mao's demotion in party ranks for infractions of discipline in the early 1930s. Mao and Chou clashed frequently on a series of issues in the period 1931-35. Chou replaced Mao as chairman of the important Military Council in 1931, but Mao took the position back after the crucial conference in 1935, which affirmed Mao's pre-eminence within the CCP. Chou, in an early demonstration of adaptability, switched sides at the decisive moment. He has worked closely with Mao ever since.

13. Over the years, however, a pattern of differences between Chou and Mao—especially as to the methods of achieving the goals of the Revolution—has been evident. Chou probably has some difficulty in fully respecting Mao in view of their strikingly dissimilar backgrounds. He probably tends to regard Mao as narrow-minded, even provincial. Nevertheless, Chou has remained the executor of Mao's ideas. His value to Mao lies in his persuasiveness and tact and his tested ability to shift from compromise to threats as the forces rallied against Mao have waxed and waned. In addition, Chou has identified himself with the power of Mao's position and exhibited his unique ability to get things done, He has been able to preserve the revolution, whereas Mao, left to his own devices, might have destroyed it.

14. Since the Communists came to power in 1949, Chou has run the government bureaucracy and has acted as the principal spokesman for the People's Republic of China before the outside world. As an administrator he appears to have few peers, and his role in making the system work has probably been huge. But the government machinery in the years before the Cultural Revolution was not the principal formulator of policy; this was the function of the party leadership. Although Chou formally ranked third in the party hierarchy, his strenqth was not in the party machinery. Indeed there is evidence that in the late 1950s and early 1960s he was in at least occasional conflict with party general secretary Teng Hsiao-ping and heir-apparent Liu Shao-chi. Thus Chou may have had good reason to side with Mao in the initial phases of the Chairman's purge of the party machine.

15. From the founding of the People's Republic of China, Chou's special province has been foreign affairs. He acted as his own foreign minister until 1958, when the late Chen I assumed the post. Real responsibility

SECRET

for the formulation (and probably execution) of policy has continued to rest with Chou, however. He has frequently shown a predilection for personal diplomacy. At Geneva in 1954, at Bandung in the following year, during several international junkets—including the famous tour of Africa in 1964, at the airport meeting with Kosygin in 1969, and most recently in his discussions with Dr. Kissinger—Chou has occupied stage center and displayed the negotiating skills honed in the difficult and extremely complex talks with the Chinese Nationalists during and immediately after the second world war. Chou has assumed many attitudes toward international problems, but he has been personally most strongly identified with those periods, such as the "Bandung era" and the present moment, when Chinese foreign policy has appeared to be most flexible and "reasonable."

16. Chou's point of view is that of an administrator, and his desire not to have things get out of hand is clearly seen in his public statements throughout the Cultural Revolution. During this period Chou was the spokesman for the government bureaucracy, which had to try to make things work in the midst of chaos. After 1967 he also appeared to speak for the party cadres, whose top leaders had been purged in the opening phases of the "revolution." In fulfilling this role Chou vigorously and publicly defended his subordinates in the government bureaucracy—he was alone among remaining regime leaders to do this. His speeches to the Red Guards in 1966 in particular provide an interesting contrast to the inflammatory tirades of Lin Piao, just then designated as Mao's heir, as well as to such members of the infamous Cultural Revolution Group (charged with overseeing the Red Guards) as Chen Po-ta and Mao's wife, Chiang Ching.

17. Chou's attempts to curb Cultural Revolution excesses (only partly successful) undoubtedly created enmity toward him in the camp of the more radically inclined. There is strong evidence that an attempt was made to purge Chou and his immediate subordinates in the spring and summer of 1967. This was at the time efforts were being made to oust important military figures in the provinces who were responsible for maintaining order once the administrative and party machinery had broken down. An alliance between Chou and these provincial military leaders was natural; they were all under attack, probably from the same quarter, and they had a common stake in maintaining a modicum of order in China. Much of Chinese political history in the past four years has revolved around the split that developed in 1967, and the greatest winner in the ensuing struggle has been Chou himself.

SECRET

18. His victory is not unalloyed, however. The ejection of Lin Piao's associates in the central military structure also entailed the removal of the chief of staff, an important figure with close ties to the provincial military leaders and to Chou himself. Several lesser members of the Cultural Revolution Group remain active, including Mao's wife, who now formally ranks just after Chou himself in the party hierarchy. There can be little doubt that Chou must look over his shoulder at these figures as he executes policy, both domestic and foreign. But his own network of allies is formidable. The ranking military man in China, Yeh Chien-ying, has been an associate of Chou since the early 1920s and has been a negotiating partner since at least the early 1940s. Chou retains ties of long standing to many important army figures; he was an instructor at the famous Whampoa Academy where many of China's military leaders were first trained and until the mid-1930s acted as political commissar for the Communist military forces. He controls the government bureaucracy and is in charge of rebuilding the party machinery, where his patronage powers will prove very useful. Moreover, because he is widely trusted, he can command considerable loyalty up and down the system.

19. The one question mark is his relationship to Mao. The Chairman has enthusiastically endorsed the purge of Chou's enemies and has emphatically set his imprimatur on the new line toward the United States. He and Chou may have agreed that the army needed curbing last autumn—Mao because the more conservative (and predominant) military elements showed obvious doubts about the wisdom of the Cultural Revolution, Chou because the overwhelming role of the army in Chinese public life violated organizational norms as he understood them. But the fact remains that Mao must have been aware of the attempt to purge Chou in 1967, and there is no evidence that he intervened decisively to defend him. Moreover, Chou has in effect been involved in a four-year quarrel with Mao's designated successor, with Mao's long-time secretary and confidant, and with Mao's wife. Mao's sense of realism, of what the "traffic can bear," seems now to have led him to heed Chou's advice in both domestic and foreign matters, but it is quite possible that Chou appreciates that Mao could turn on him. In the worst of conflicts since 1935, however, Chou has consistently displayed personal loyalty to Mao, whatever their policy differences, and this may continue to stand him in good stead.

PART II
Teng Hsiao-p'ing: A Profile

Central Intelligence Agency
Directorate of Intelligence
April 8, 1974

Intelligence Memorandum
Teng Hsiao-p'ing: A Profile

Member, Politburo, Chinese Communist Party Central Committee; Vice Premier, State Council.

The second highest ranking victim of the Cultural Revolution (1966–69), Teng (pronounced dung) Hsiaop'ing returned to public life as a Vice Premier of the State Council in April, 1973. Elected to the 10th Central Committee of the Chinese Communist Party (CCP-CC) in August 1973, Teng was promoted to the Politburo in January 1974. In addition, he apparently became the only civilian member of the Military Commission of the CCP-CC.

The most active and prominent of the rehabilitated victims of the Cultural Revolution, Teng has maintained a heavy schedule of meetings with foreigners and has served as the primary escort of visiting Chiefs of State during their tours of China. Relieving Premier Chou En-lai of many routine daily responsibilities, Teng has probably become a supporter of the moderate Premier in the delicate balance between radicals and moderates within the Politburo.

Teng 's prestigious assignment to head China's delegation to the UN General Assembly Special Session on World Resources in April 1974 has made him the highest level Chinese official to visit the United States since the founding of the People's Republic of China (PRC) in 1949.

Fall From Power

By January 1965 Teng ranked third in power after CCP Chairman Mao Tsetung and the newly elected President of the PRC, Liu Shao-ch'i; the latter two controlled the party and state apparatus, respectively. Teng had been a Vice Premier since 1952 and secretary general of the party and a member of the Politburo since 1954.

Late in 1965 Mao, alarmed by the ideological weakening of the leadership and the masses, launched the Cultural Revolution. One year later Teng and Liu, charged with responsibility for the ideological backsliding, were disgraced and removed from their posts.

Mao's principal complaint against Teng was that he failed to keep him informed and relied for advice on such critics of Mao as the mayor of Peking, P'eng Chen. In retrospect, Teng may have been guilty of little more. In his confession of October 1966 he admitted being guilty only of bureaucratism and subjectivism making decisions without a scientific analysis of Marxist-Leninist Mao Tse-tung Thought. Teng was never criticized in official public media, and responsible critics never questioned his patriotism. Teng's last public appearance before his rehabilitation was. in December 1966. His name was seldom mentioned after 1969, while Liu Shao-ch'i's remained a common epithet.

Rehabilitation

By 1969 rumors had already begun to circulate that Teng would return to official circles, and by 1972 several reports placed him in a low-level party office in- Peking. It was probably in 1972 that Mao, over the opposition of his wife, Chiang Ch'ing, who leads the radical faction in the Politburo, but with the concurrence of Premier Chou En-lai, leader of the moderate faction, endorsed the reversal of the party's judgment of Teng. Teng's confession to serious errors, his proven organizational expertise, and his past record of loyalty to the party and to Mao combined to win him his reinstatement.

Debate over the rehabilitation of Teng and other victims of the Cultural Revolution has deepened the split between the moderate and radical factions within the Politburo. There is still significant opposition to Teng's return from leaders who came to power as a result of the Cultural Revolution. Chiang Ch'ing, who was conspicuously absent from the state banquet at which Teng - former target of her verbal assaults - made his first public appearance in 1973, waited nearly 2 months before making a joint appearance with him. She is probably responsible for the periodic attacks in China's media on moves, including the rehabilitation of purged officials, that have tended to subvert Cultural Revolution accomplishments.

Early Life and Career

Teng Hsiao-p'ing was born in Szechwan Province on 22 August 1904. He graduated from a middle school in his native province. In about 1919 he went to Shanghai, where he joined a worker-student group that included such prominent Chinese Communists as Chou En-lai, Li Li-san, Nieh Jung-chen, Ch'en I,

Li Wei-han, Ts'ai Ch'ang and Li Fu-ch'un. In 1920 this group went to France to receive higher education and to assist in postwar French reconstruction. While in Paris Teng and his colleagues founded the Chinese Communist Youth Party in 1921.

After spending a few months in the Soviet Union, Teng returned to China in about 1926 and joined the CCP. He subsequently worked on party organization matters in Shanghai until the CCP-Kuomintang (KMT) split in 1927. During the next 3 years he helped organize army units to fight against the KMT during the Chinese civil war. In the Kiangsi Soviet in 1931, Teng was a section chief in the Propaganda Department, an editor of the army journal Hung Hsing (Red Star) and a teacher at the Red Army Academy at Jui-chin. In 1934-35 he took part in the Long March to Shensi Province. During the Sino-Japanese War (1937-45) Teng was the political commissar of the famous 129th Division of the 8th Route Army. By the end of World War II he had become one of the most important political figures in the Red Army.

When he was elected to the CCP-CC in 1945, Teng was a member of the North China Bureau of the CCP-CC and political commissar of the military districts in that area. Shortly after the establishment of the People's Republic of China in October 1949, Teng became a member of the new Central People's Government, the People's Revolutionary Military Council and the National Committee of the Chinese People's Political Consultative Conference (CPPCC); he retained those posts until the government reorganization of September 1954. With the establishment of the Southwest Bureau in 1950, he emerged as a ranking party official. Headquartered in Chungking, he served until 1952 as secretary of the bureau, as political commissar of the Southwest Military District and as vice chairman of the Southwest Military and Administrative Committee.

Transferred to Peking in August 1952, Teng was appointed a Vice Premier and given a seat on the State Planning Commission (SPC). In September 1953 he succeeded Po I-po as Minister of Finance and also became a vice chairman of the Finance and Economics Committee.

He abruptly lost both of these posts in June 1954 when he became secretary general of the CCP. With the reorganization of the government later that year, Teng remained a Vice Premier and assumed the additional position of Vice Chairman of the National Defense Council. In addition, he was a Standing Committee member of the Second CPPCC (1954–59).

The Kao Kang Conspiracy

Circumstantial evidence linked Teng' s sudden shift to the post of secretary general of the CCP in 1954 to the purge of Politburo Member and Chairman of the SPC Kao Kang, CCP-CC Organization Department Director Jao Shu-shih and others who were involved in what was described as an antiparty alliance. As a member of the SPC, Teng had been in a good position to learn of Kao's plot to overthrow the leadership and might even have been asked to join the conspiracy. In 1955 Teng delivered the CCP-CC report on the uncovered conspiracy, suggesting that he had been instrumental in foiling the antiparty plot. Shortly after delivering the report, Teng was elected to the Politburo.

One year later Teng emerged as one of the enormously powerful members of the small inner circle of party leaders when, during the Eighth Party Congress, he gave one of the three major addresses—the report on the revised party constitution. Formerly the lowest ranking member of a 10-man Politburo, he then rose to become sixth ranked in a 26-man Politburo and was named to its Standing Committee. He was also named general secretary of the party, a post that had been vacant since the 1920s, and head of the party's Secretariat, a collective group charged with running the daily affairs of the party.

Teng did not associate himself with the Hundred Flowers movement of early 1957 that exploded into criticism of the CCP. When the rectification campaign began later that year, however, Teng was placed in charge. Delivering the key address to the Third Plenum of the Eighth Party Congress, he defended the party and suggested policies to rectify the short-comings that had surfaced during the Hundred Flowers movement.

During 1958–59 Teng also managed to avoid close association with the disastrous Great Leap Forward, Mao's effort to rapidly industrialize China's economy. Apparently critical of the excesses of that campaign, Teng nevertheless wrote a defense of the program that appeared in Jen-min Jih-pao (People's Daily) and in a special collection of PRC 10th anniversary materials. When Defense Minister P'eng Te-huai and other alleged covert critics of Mao and the Great Leap were purged, Teng was not adversely affected.

Teng was a delegate to each of the. National People's Congresses, held in 1954, 1959 and 1964.

Soviet Baiter

Teng's extensive liaison activity with foreign Communist parties, particularly the Communist Party of the Soviet Union (CPSU), played an important role in enhancing his prestige during the 1950s. In October 1954 he was a member of the CCP group that discussed Sino-Soviet relations and the international situation with the Soviet delegation to the PRC headed by Premier Nikita Khrushchev. He attended the 20th Congress of the CPSU in Moscow in 1956 and subsequently played a prominent part in the Sino-Soviet talks held in Peking with the Soviet delegation led by Anastas Mikoyan.

In 1957 Teng accompanied Mao to Moscow, where the Communist parties of the world negotiated the first of the Moscow Declarations on party unity. At the Second Session of the Eighth CCP Party Congress in May 1958, Teng delivered the party report on the Moscow meeting and earned the accolade, "Mao Tse-tung's close comrade in arms," an honor reserved for only five others in the party's history.

As the Sino-Soviet rift began to emerge in the late 1950's and early 1960's, Teng continued to play a pivotal role in Sino-Soviet relations. He was a key figure in the activities surrounding Khrushchev's 1959 visit to Peking. In 1960 Teng returned to the Soviet Union for the 43rd anniversary of the October Revolution and a November summit meeting of SinoSoviet leaders. The Chinese and the Russians criticized each other severely at the summit sessions. Teng, even though he was deputy head of the delegation led by CCP Vice Chairman Liu Shao-ch'i, made his country's major speeches. In an unpublicized meeting with Premier Khrushchev, Teng forcefully accused the CPSU of developing a new personality cult around the Soviet Premier and of weakening the international Communist movement. In addition, he reputedly defended Mao against Khrushchev's criticism and charged the CPSU with attempting to subvert the Chinese leadership.

After the capitulation of the USSR to the United States in the Cuban missile crisis and its failure to support the PRC in the Sino-Indian border war in 1962, Sino-soviet relations worsened. Teng, who by then had earned the reputation of being a man able to stand up to and infuriate the Kremlin, again went to Moscow to meet Khrushchev in July 1963. Upon his departure from Peking he received an unprecedented sendoff, attended by nearly every major Chinese leader. After 2 fruitless weeks of negotiations, Teng returned to Peking and a welcome that gave an equally impressive demonstration of Chinese unity.

Before the Cultural Revolution Teng was addicted to the game of bridge, flying in bridge partners from around the country in army aircraft. His only known foreign language is French.

Teng has been married twice. His second wife, Cho Lin, is not politically active. According to Red Guard sources the couple has three daughters.

8 April 1974

COSIMO is a specialty publisher for independent authors, not-for-profit organizations, and innovative businesses, dedicated to publishing books that inspire, inform, and engage readers around the world.

Our mission is to create a smart and sustainable society by connecting people with valuable ideas. We offer authors and organizations full publishing support, while using the newest technologies to present their works in the most timely and effective way.

COSIMO BOOKS offers fine books that inspire, inform and engage readers on a variety of subjects, including personal development, socially responsible business, economics and public affairs.

COSIMO CLASSICS brings to life unique and rare classics, representing a wide range of subjects that include Business, Economics, History, Personal Development, Philosophy, Religion & Spirituality, and much more!

COSIMO REPORTS publishes reports that affect your world, from global trends to the economy, and from health to geopolitics.

COSIMO B2B offers custom editions for historical societies, museums, companies and other organizations interested in offering classic books to their audiences, customized with their own logo and message. **COSIMO B2B** also offers publishing services to organizations, such as media firms, think tanks, conference organizers and others who could benefit from having their own imprint.